Hammerhead Sharks

Victoria Blakemore

Copyright info/picture credits

Cover, frantisek hojdysz/AdobeStock; Page 3, Ilan Ben Tov/AdobeStock; Page 5, Mark/AdobeStock; Page 7, wildestanimal/AdobeStock; Page 9, niritman/Pixabay; Pages 10-11, Pexels/Pixabay; Page 13, momof2littlegirls/Pixabay; Page 15, Mark/AdobeStock; Page 17, SadBoyPro/AdobeStock; Page 19, Michael Shake/AdobeStock; Page 21, steffstarr/AdobeStock; Page 23; hakbak/AdobeStock; Page 25, Marion Kraschl/AdobeStock; Page 27, frantisek hojdysz/AdobeStock; Page 29, kitti bowornphatnon/AdobeStock; Page 31, frantisek hojdysz/AdobeStock; Page 33, b.neeser/AdobeStock

Table of Contents

Hammerhead sharks are large fish that are known for the **unique** shape of their head.

There are nine kinds of hammerhead sharks. They differ in size and where they live.

Hammerhead sharks are usually

gray, brown, and white in color.

They can look a little green in

some waters. 3

Size

Most kinds of hammerhead shark can grow to be about thirteen feet long. The great hammerhead shark can be up to twenty feet long.

Hammerheads can grow to weigh up to 1,000 pounds, although most are smaller.

The great hammerhead

shark is the largest of the

nine kinds of hammerheads.

Physical Characteristics

Hammerheads have a wide, narrow head. It is very different from other sharks.

The wide, front part of a hammerhead shark's head has special sensors on it. These sensors are called the ampullae of lorenzini. They help the shark to sense prey that is nearby.

A hammerhead shark's eyes are on the two sides of it's head. This helps it to see farther around it's body.

7

Habitat

Hammerhead sharks are usually found in tropical waters. They may **migrate** to cooler waters in the summer.

They are often seen in shallow waters, but can also be found farther from shore.

Range

Hammerhead sharks can be found in the oceans around all continents except Antarctica.

The Arctic ocean and the waters around Antarctica are too cold for hammerhead sharks.

Diet

Hammerhead sharks are **carnivores**. This means that they only eat meat.

Their diet is made up of stingrays, fish, crabs, squid, lobsters, and other sea creatures. Their preferred prey is stingrays.

Hammerhead sharks often feed
on stingrays. They are usually
found on the ocean floor.

Hammerhead sharks trap prey on the ocean floor when they are hunting.

Their mouth is located on the bottom side of their head. The location of their mouth makes it easier for them to eat prey that they have trapped with their head.

Hammerhead sharks usually

hunt alone.

Communication

Unlike many other animals,

sharks are unable to make

sounds. Their communication

is mainly through movement.

Hammerhead sharks have

been known to arch their body

to send signals to other sharks.

Researchers are still learning about how sharks communicate. It can be hard to study because many sharks spend their time alone.

Movement

Hammerheads spend most of their time swimming at one or two miles per hour. When needed, they can swim up to twenty-five miles per hour.

Hammerheads are very **agile**. They are able to turn quickly.

Hammerheads, like other kinds

of sharks, cannot swim

backwards.

Hammerhead Pups

Hammerhead sharks may have anywhere between five and sixty pups.

Newborn pups have a more rounded head than their parents. It will change shape and flatten as they grow.

Hammerhead shark pups

usually leave their mother

right after they are born.

Hammerhead Life

Hammerhead sharks are usually **solitary** animals. They are often alone.

However, they are sometimes seen travelling together in large groups, or schools.

When they are in schools, it is

often because they are

migrating to warmer waters.

Feeding Sharks

There are some companies that bring divers out to areas where they can feed sharks.

Some people think that feeding sharks is good. They say that it helps the sharks and makes people more aware of what sharks are really like.

Other people do not like the idea of feeding sharks. They say that sharks may begin to think of food when they see divers. It could be dangerous for divers.

Population

Two of the nine kinds of

hammerhead sharks are

endangered. All hammerhead

shark populations have been

declining.

If hammerhead sharks are not

helped, they may soon be

extinct.

In the wild, hammerhead sharks

may live between twenty and

thirty years.

Hammerhead Sharks in Danger

Like many other sharks,

hammerhead sharks are

hunted for their fins, meat,

and hides.

Many times, they are caught

only for their fins, which are

used in shark fin soup.

Shark fin soup is a **delicacy** in some countries. The soup is made from the fins of sharks like hammerheads.

Helping Hammerhead Sharks

There are laws that protect
sharks from being caught for
their fins.

People are educating others
about shark fins and products
that have shark oil. They are
trying to keep sharks from being
hunted.

Shark habitats are being **polluted**. By recycling, we can help to keep their habitats free from trash.

Special conservation zones are areas that are protected from fishing and hunting sharks. They provide sharks with a safe habitat.

Glossary

Agile: able to move quickly

Carnivore: an animal that
eats only meat

Declining: getting smaller

Delicacy: a food that is rare
and special

Endangered: at risk of
becoming extinct

Extinct: when there are no
more of an animal left

Migrate: when an animal travels from one place to another

Polluted: full of waste or garbage

Solitary: living without others, alone

Unique: different, special

About the Author

Victoria Blakemore is a first grade

teacher in Southwest Florida with a

passion for reading.

You can visit her at

www.elementaryexplorers.com

Also in This Series

Gray Wolves	Sloths	Flamingos	Camels	Koalas	Honey Bees	Pandas
Pangolins	White-Tailed Deer	Orcas	Giraffes	Corn	Meerkats	Echidnas
Walruses	Raccoons	Bald Eagles	Apples	Arctic Foxes	Red Pandas	Cassowaries
Tigers	Ladybugs	Moose	Beluga Whales	Leopards	Elephants	Jellyfish
Binturongs	Lions	Dolphins	Reindeer	Hammerhead Sharks	Hippos	Pumpkins
Peafowl	Chameleons	Florida Panthers	Aye-Ayes	Black Bears	Cheetahs	Manatees
Gingerbread	Polar Bears	Hot Chocolate	Orangutans	Coyotes	Marshmallows	Strawberries

Also in This Series

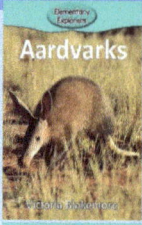

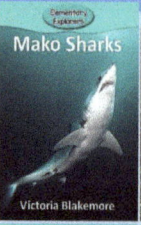

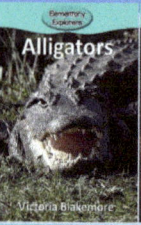

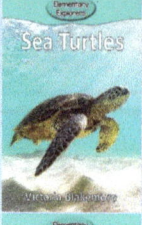

Aardvarks	Mako Sharks	Alligators	Frogs	Hedgehogs	Brown Bears	Bongos
Sea Turtles	Quokkas	Muskrats	Zebras	Red Foxes	Ring-Tailed Lemurs	Platypuses
Anteaters	Kangaroos	Rhinos	Jaguars	Wombats	Capybaras	Gorillas
Cats	Skunks	Butterflies	Dingoes	Snow Leopards	African Wild Dogs	Penguins
Whale Sharks	Wolverines	Warthogs	Caracals	Badgers	Seals	Hummingbird
Pikas	Humpback Whales	Pumas	Lemonade	Llamas	Tulips	Ostriches
Sunflowers	Fennec Foxes	Sea Lions	Squirrels	Roses	Porcupines	Ice Cream

All titles by Victoria Blakemore